This book is available as a personalised story, customised with a choice of name and physical characteristics.

To see our full range go to:

www.thestoryof-books.com

Copyright © Kate Polley. The right of Kate Polley to be identified as the author of this work has been asserted in accordance with the Copyright, Designs and Patents Act. All rights reserved.
First published in the UK in 2014 by:

The Solopreneur Publishing Company Ltd.
West Yorkshire WF9 1PB

The publisher makes no representation, expressed or implied, with regards to the accuracy of the information contained in this book, and cannot accept any responsibility or liability.

Except for the quotation of small passages for the purposes of criticism and review, no part of this publication may be reproduced, stored in a retrieval system, or transmitted, in any form or by any means, electronic, mechanical, photocopying, recording or otherwise, except under the terms of the Copyright, Designs and Patents Act 1988 without the prior consent of the publisher at the address above.

Printed in the U.K.

This book is based on the story 'Sam and Finn' which was originally written about my twin sons, Samuel and Finn Polley after Sam's death.

It is a story of hope which will remind you that we can experience the love and joy of a loved one, even when they are no longer with us here on earth.

"Love is like life, merely longer' – Emily Dickinson

Kate Polley lives in Cape Town, South Africa, together with her husband Peter and their children, Hannah, Erin, Finn and Jude.

Contact email: info@thestoryof-books.com

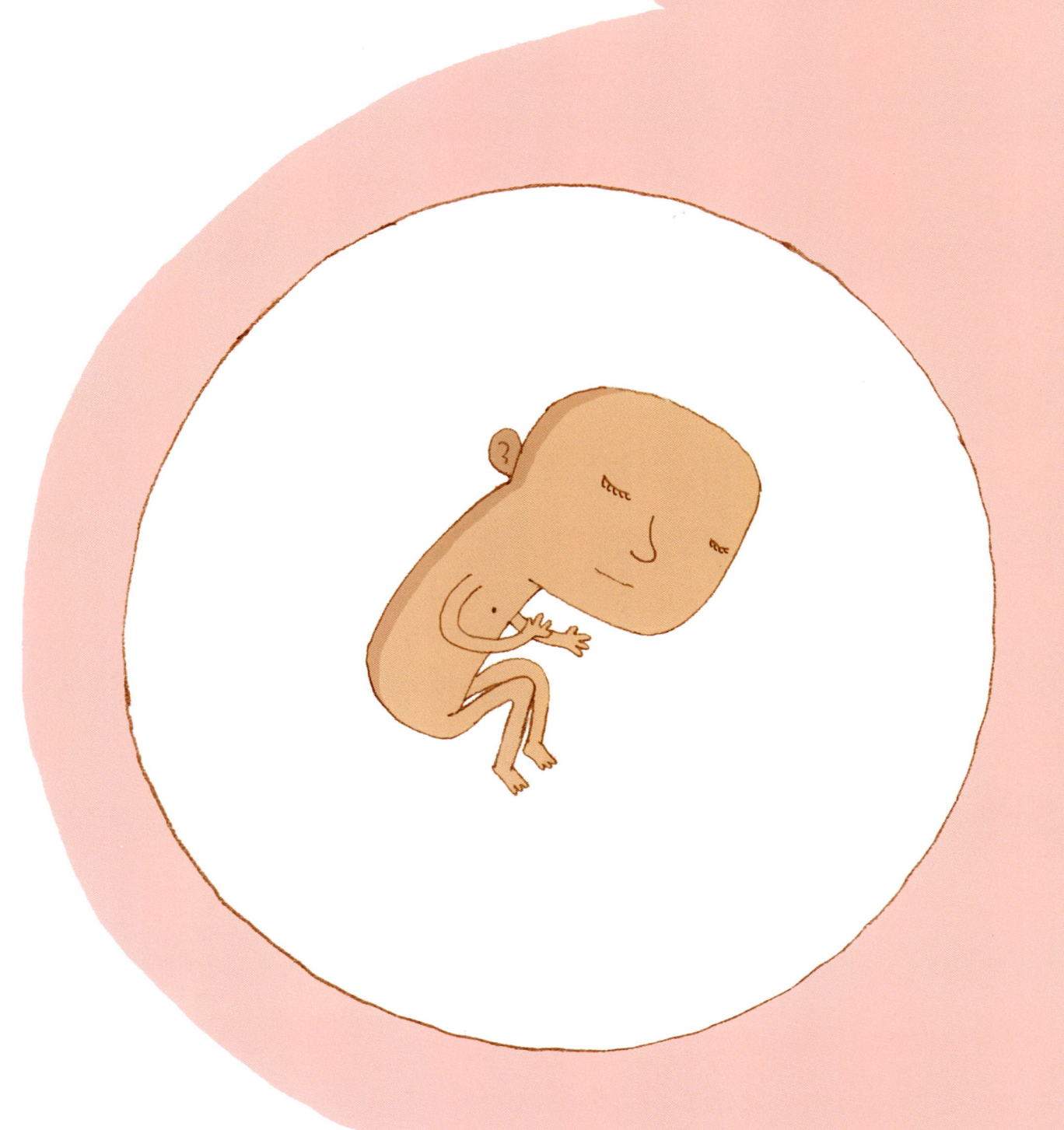

This is the story of my baby sister,
who even though we cannot see...

Lives within you and me!

When my baby sister was no longer strong,

it was time for her to move along.

Before she had to say goodbye,

she whispered gently:

It's OK to cry.

Even though I cannot stay,

I will still be with you every day.

Whilst the time has come for me to go,

I love you more than you'll ever know.

I am the brightest star in the night sky,

a butterfly flapping way up high.

I am the dancing summer breeze,

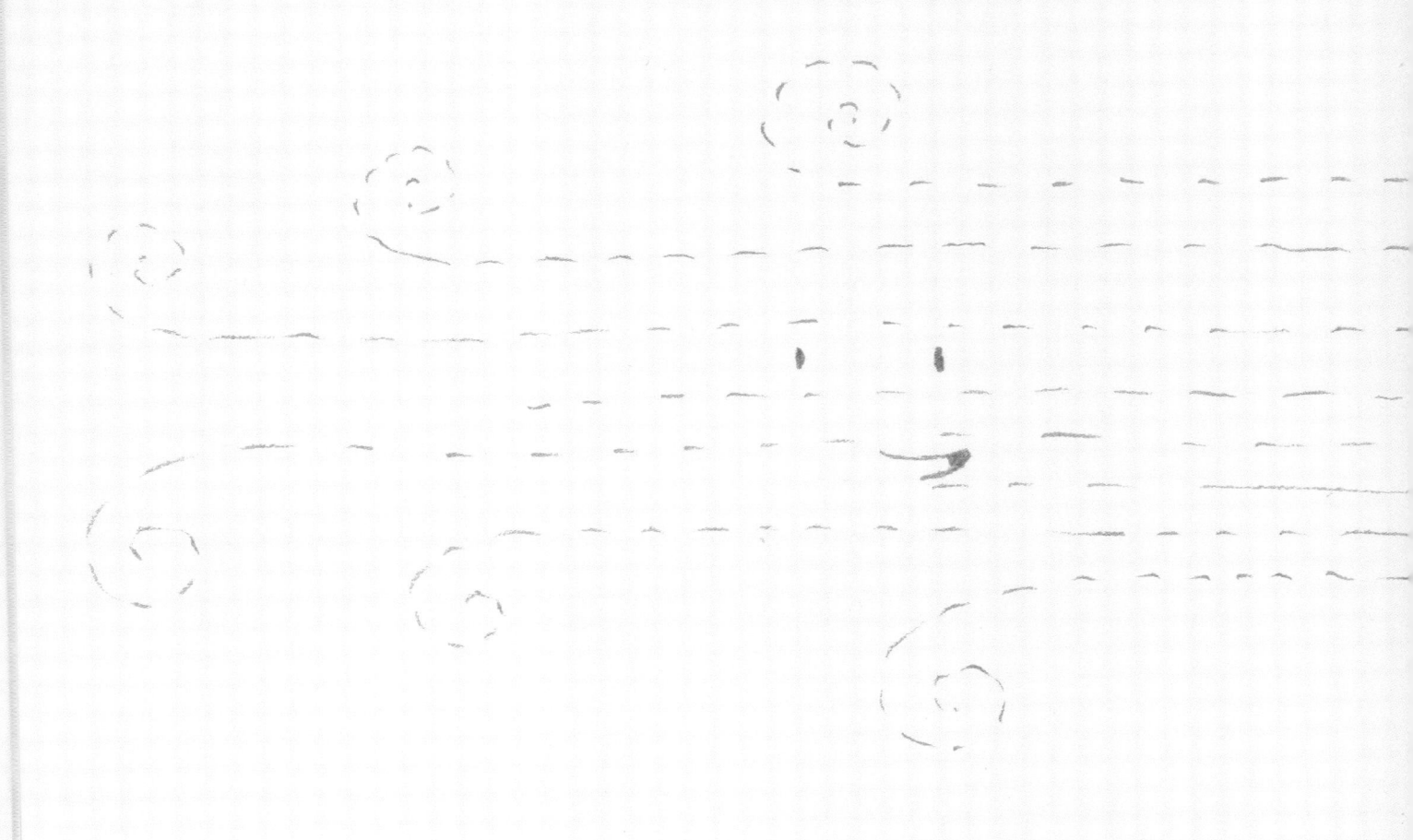

and the golden autumn leaves.

I am the sand that tickles your toes,

and the sun that kisses your nose.

I am the sparkle in your eye,

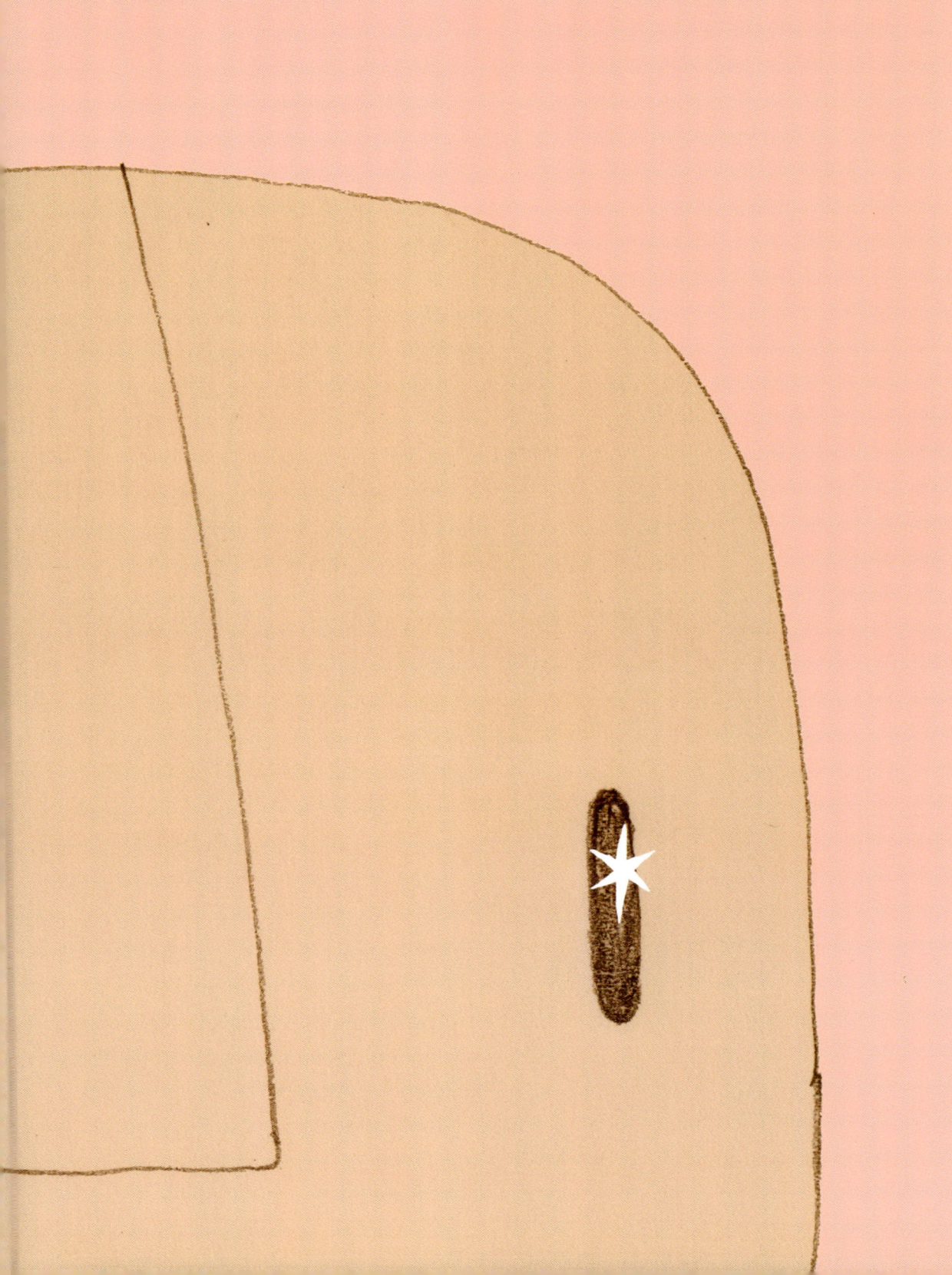

and the salty tears you cry.

I am the dimple in your cheek,

and your grubby little feet.

I am the soft curl of your hair,

and the depth of your twinkly eyed stare.

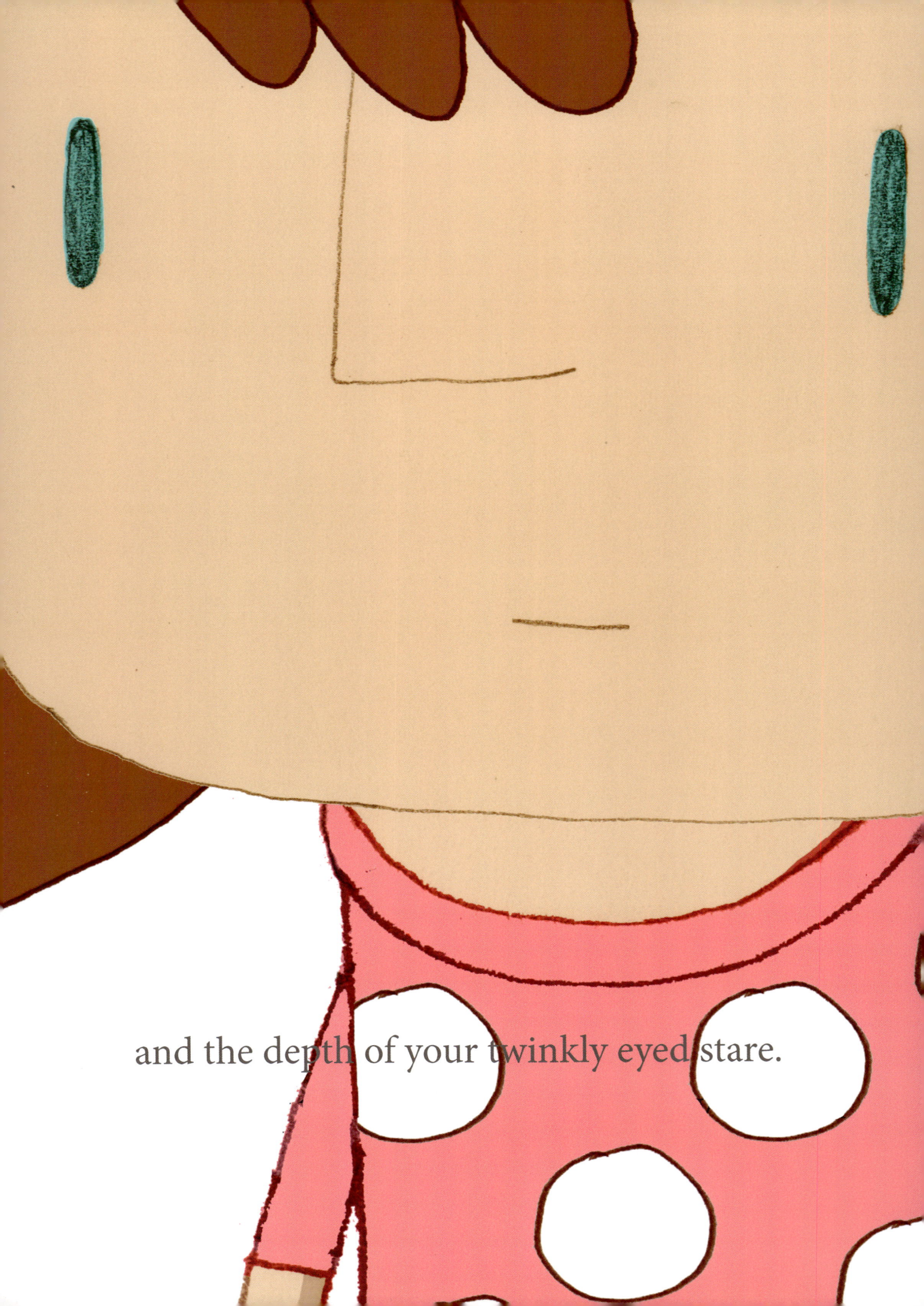

I am the gurgle in your laughter,

burp!

I am your ... forever after.

Your loving baby sister I will always be.

So when you feel lonely or just a bit blue,

take a moment and think of me.

Look all around you and right on cue...

I'll be smiling back at you!

THE END